Hidden Worlds
Amazing Tunnel Stories

by Debora Pearson

art • Tina Holdcroft

Annick Press Ltd.

Toronto   Vancouver

Annick Press Ltd.

We acknowledge the support of the Canada Council for the Arts, the Ontario Arts Council, and the Government of Canada through the Book Publishing Industry Development Program (BPIDP) for our publishing activities.

Cataloging in Publication Data

Pearson, Debora
    Hidden worlds : amazing tunnel stories

ISBN 1-55037-745-0 (bound).—ISBN 1-55037-744-2 (pbk.)

1. Tunneling—Juvenile literature. 2. Tunnels—Juvenile literature. I. Holdcroft, Tina II. Title.

TA807.P42 2002   j624.1'93   C2002-901128-0

The art in this book was rendered in watercolor.
The text was typeset in Clearface, Officina, and Smile.

Distributed in Canada by:
Firefly Books Ltd.
3680 Victoria Park Avenue
Willowdale, ON
M2H 3K1

Published in the U.S.A. by Annick Press (U.S.) Ltd.
Distributed in the U.S.A. by:
Firefly Books (U.S.) Inc.
P.O. Box 1338
Ellicott Station
Buffalo, NY 14205

Manufactured in China.

visit us at: www.annickpress.com

Kids should never dig
their own tunnels.
Digging a tunnel can
be an extremely
dangerous activity, as
the tunnel may collapse.

For my nephew, Daniel Vanderkaden.
Dig in and enjoy! — D.P.

For Tom Morgan. — T.H.

Contents

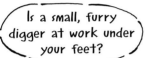

Introduction

A tunnel is full of mysteries and secrets ...

Hidden deep in the ground beneath your feet, a hollowed-out passage stretches off in the distance. This is a tunnel. Who knows where it leads to, or what's inside it ...

A tunnel can go almost anywhere. It can cut through a rock-filled mountain or wind under city streets. It can lead to a castle or run inside a pyramid. It can be an escape route, or a shortcut to water, or even a burial ground.

A tunnel is an amazing place, a hidden world filled with mysteries and secrets. It could be a home for a mole, a path for a train, or a speedy way to deliver the mail!

In this book you can peer inside some remarkable tunnels and discover their stories – why they were made, where they are found, and who has used them. All of the stories, except for the myth of the Minotaur's Labyrinth, are true tales, about real-life tunnels.

So get set to plunge into a salt mine, explore the Great Pyramid, and burrow out of a prison camp – with the help of tunnels, you can do it all!

Dark, Cozy Mole Holes

It's a warm, sunny Saturday in the spring and everyone's at the park. Kids call out to each other as they climb the monkey bars and ride on the swings. Others laugh and cheer as they kick a soccer ball over the grass.

Everyone's playing, having fun in the sun – everyone, that is, except a strange little digger at work underground. It's an eastern mole, found in parts of North America, and it hurries through its network of tunnels buried under the park. It's busy carving out a dark, cozy place where it will tend its babies after they're born. Although this mammal is as small as a chipmunk and weighs as little as two chocolate bars when it's full-grown, it's also a mighty excavator – it can tunnel the length of a car in just one hour.

Tunneling is difficult work and the mole is hungry. It uses its long, pointy nose like a finger to feel around for food. Aha! Another tiny tunneler – an earthworm – is burrowing nearby. The mole seizes the worm in its paws, bites off its head to keep it from wriggling, and gulps it down. Then the mole scurries off. Snack time is over: it's time to start digging again!

These tunnels are used for finding worms and other food. To make the tunnels, the mole "swims" through the earth, using its nails like tiny shovels to scoop away dirt.

It presses the loose dirt on the roof of the tunnel, making ridges that you can see above the ground.

To make these tunnels, the mole "dives" into the earth and sweeps the dirt under and behind its body.

Then it turns around and pushes the earth back up to the surface, where it forms a tiny mountain called a molehill.

Deeper tunnels are used for raising babies and for living in, especially during the cold winter months.

An Old Old Tunnel Tale

What would it be like to enter some dark, winding tunnels without being sure that you will ever find your way out of them again? And what if you had to track down a fierce monster that lives in the tunnels and kill it – before it kills you? All these things happen in a made-up story about tunnels that people have told for thousands of years …

The tunnels in this tale were found in the Labyrinth, a confusing maze of passageways that lay underground, near the palace of King Minos, on the island of Crete. In the center of the Labyrinth lived the Minotaur, a ferocious being, half human and half bull, that ate people.

Each year, King Minos sent some men and women into the Labyrinth to be devoured by the Minotaur. None of them escaped. Then a brave man named Theseus came along. He was able to kill the Minotaur *and* find a way out of the Labyrinth.

One of King Minos's daughters, Ariadne, showed Theseus the secret to getting out. To find out more, look to the right. Then see if you can help Theseus find a way to the Minotaur. But watch out – the Labyrinth is filled with many dead ends, and the Minotaur is getting restless!

Answer on page 28

> Here, Theseus, take this ball of thread and unwind it as you walk. To find your way out, just follow the trail of thread back here.

> Thanks, Ariadne! Now if I can just find the Minotaur before it finds me …

8

Make Way for the Water!

The people who live in ancient Rome are proud of their city. It has many lovely fountains overflowing with sparkling water, and public baths where everyone flocks to exercise, bathe, and visit their friends. There is just one problem: each day the fountains and public baths use huge amounts of water. Thousands of people live in Rome and they need water too, for drinking. There isn't enough fresh water near the city for all the people, fountains, and baths.

But far away, out in the country, there *is* lots of water. It has collected in springs

found high in the mountains, and this water is clear and pure, perfect for drinking and bathing. But the Romans don't have a way to get the water to their city – until they build an aqueduct.

An aqueduct is a long channel, or path, that starts at the springs and carries water downhill to Rome, where the aqueduct ends. Parts of it consist of bridges that run above-ground, over valleys. But most of an aqueduct is carved through earth and solid rock. The ancient Romans are excellent tunnel builders: one aqueduct has tunnels that run underground for 50 miles (81 kilometers). It would take a person over two days to walk that distance!

11

Pyramid Secrets

The fierce sun beats down on the men mounted on camels, but the men hardly notice. They're staring at the huge stone-block mountain that looms before them. Next to it, they feel tinier than ants. This is the Great Pyramid of Giza, the largest stone structure ever made.

By the time these men have arrived here – in Egypt, more than a thousand years ago – the Great Pyramid is already very, very old. It was built 3,000 years before as the burial place of King Khufu, one of the pharaohs who ruled ancient Egypt.

The men on the camels have heard about a passageway hidden inside the pyramid that leads to a room filled with jewels and riches. It is said that the Great Pyramid holds other treasures too: scientific secrets that the ancient Egyptians once knew, secrets now lost and forgotten.

Today, the men are in search of that secret knowledge. Their ruler, Caliph al-Mamun of Baghdad, an educated man who loves science, has ordered them to find the pyramid's tunnel and bring back the treasure.

The men break into the Great Pyramid and discover mysterious passageways and rooms. But they are too late to find anything else. The treasure – whatever it was – is long gone.

The inside of the pyramid was completely filled in with stone blocks — except for open areas like this tunnel (right) and the two upper rooms. The pyramid workers carefully planned where these spaces would be, then built around them.

I love a good secret!

Attack the Castle!

The time: almost 800 years ago, in the days when knights fought in battles. A castle stands on a hilltop in England. This is Rochester Castle, a fortress in the land ruled by King John.

Rochester Castle is a safe place for King John's subjects to live in: it has thick stone walls, and there's only one main way in and out, through a gateway that is sealed up during times of war. No one can break into this fortress … or can they?

While King John and his army are away at war, some of his enemies come to Rochester. They convince the man left in charge of the castle to turn it over to them. When King John returns, he discovers that Rochester is filled with intruders. To get the castle back, he'll have to break into it.

King John tries using rock-throwing machines to crash through the castle walls, but the walls are too strong. Then he has an idea: attack the castle underground. Miners dig tunnels under the castle towers and prop wooden beams there. When they set the wood on fire, the tunnels will collapse, toppling the towers. Part of mighty Rochester is about to fall – all because of King John's tunnels.

15

A World of Salt

A miner chips away at the rocky, white crystals on the wall before him. Thud! A chunk falls to the ground and the miner picks it up. In the light of his torch, the heavy rock looks like rough, dusty glass. He's holding a block of salt – and all around him, deep in this mine, there's salt as far as he can see.

Over six hundred years ago, during the time of this miner, salt was almost as valuable as gold. People couldn't survive without salt. It helped them stay healthy and it kept their food from going bad. Salt was important – and it wasn't always easy to find.

But at the Wieliczka (Vye-LEECH-ka) mine in Poland, where this miner works, there is salt: a huge deposit has been found underground. To reach the salt, men carve long, snaking tunnels through the earth. Over time, the mine grows big and very busy. It becomes a vast world of salt.

Its tunnels run for hundreds of miles. Some tunnels lead down to saltwater lakes and large chambers where horses, hitched to treadmills, pull up loads of salt. Other tunnels are connected to underground churches with glittering chandeliers and beautiful statues – many of them made entirely of salt.

Salt!

Today, people come to this underground church (below) to pray, get married, or listen to concerts that are performed here.

16

Beneath Paris Streets ...

The sun is setting over the city of Paris. Soon it will be night. But here, in the tunnels that run under the city, it's always nighttime. The tunnels lie 66 feet (20 meters) deep in the ground, far from any sunlight. It's cool and quiet here – and very dark.

This is the place where miners found the rock used to make the city's buildings and walls. To reach the rock, the miners made quarries by hollowing out the ground and digging long tunnels and huge chambers in the earth. Now, near the end of the 18th century, some tunnels are over 600 years old. Their walls are crumbling; the ground above them is caving in.

For the first time in years, workers enter the quarries. They've come here to repair and strengthen the tunnels before they cause more damage. As the men walk

Five million and ten, five million and eleven ...

The empty tunnels and chambers were turned into burial grounds over 200 years ago. For many nights, beginning at dusk, bones from the overcrowded cemeteries were placed on carts, brought underground, and stacked in neat piles. More than six million skeletons were carried here.

through the roomy passageways and chambers, they gaze about in amazement. There's so much empty, unused space here!

Above-ground, in the crowded city, there's a shortage of space. Even the cemeteries are running out of room to bury the dead. Some cemeteries are so crammed, people say, that skeletons poke out of the ground. New burial grounds are needed – and they must be found fast.

The people of Paris decide that the patched-up quarries are the perfect place for a new cemetery. Skeletons from the overflowing cemeteries are brought underground. As other people die, they're buried here too. Soon this calm, still place, called the Paris Catacombs, holds millions of bones.

The ancient Romans were the first to excavate the ground where Paris now stands. When they occupied this area, over 2,000 years ago, the Romans dug quarries and used the rock they found to make buildings and walls.

Beginning about 900 years ago, long after the Romans left, the people of Paris tunneled deeper into the ground. Today, a great silent world exists under the city — its tunnels and chambers are over 186 miles (300 kilometers) long.

I'd better fix this tunnel wall before it caves in ...

In some places it's so wet that water drips gently down on the bones.

A Shy Man Hides

A strangely dressed gentleman, wearing a very tall hat, two coats, and three pairs of socks, and holding a large umbrella, hurries into a tunnel. He is the fifth Duke of Portland, a wealthy man who lived over a century ago. The tunnel runs under his home, a grand country house called Welbeck Abbey, in England.

People who live near Welbeck have heard about its owner and his peculiar appearance, but they rarely ever see him. His Grace, as the Duke is known, is extremely shy. And he has come up with an unusual way to avoid meeting people: he has had tunnels dug beneath his property. His Grace uses these passageways to go from his house to places nearby without being seen.

Today, he is about to leave Welbeck for his city home in far-off London. To get there, he will enter a carriage that takes him underground to the train station. There, the carriage – with His Grace still inside – will be loaded onto the train for London. His trip will be so private, so secret, that hardly anyone will know he has left Welbeck.

But in his hurry to reach his carriage, the Duke of Portland has dropped his umbrella and top hat. As well, four handkerchiefs and a pair of socks have fallen out of his pockets. Can you find them somewhere in the tunnels?

Answer on page 30

The Duke of Portland built a huge underground ballroom here. No one is sure why His Grace did this – he didn't like throwing parties!

Some underground rooms even had skylights in their ceilings to let in sunlight from above ground.

21

Tunnels for Tiny Trains

In the city of Chicago, 90 years ago, the streets are packed with crowded streetcars and noisy automobiles, a recent invention. There are horses too, pulling wagonloads of coal, which is used to heat all the buildings. Everyone's in a hurry, but no one gets anywhere fast because of all the traffic jams. It can take hours for a horse and wagon to travel several short blocks.

But under the streets, beneath the sewers, there's a secret route for getting around quickly: long, skinny tunnels that criss-cross the city. There are no streetcars here, or horses, or automobiles – just dozens of hard-working trains.

Compared with the huge trains that zoom between cities, these ones are small – their cars are just the width of a bathtub. They look like something you'd find at an amusement park, the kind of train you

The trains ran on electricity. A trolley pole on top of each locomotive received power from an electrical wire that ran along the ceiling.

Oops! There goes my map. I'm lost without it!

Each locomotive was so small that it could hold just one person, the motorman. He couldn't stand up while he ran the train — he would have hit his head on the ceiling or got an electrical shock from the wire above him!

CHICAGO TUNNELS MAP

might like to ride on just for fun.

The trains may be kid-size, but they tackle big jobs. They haul freights cars filled with coal and other cargo to buildings, making deliveries faster than horses or trucks. The trains work day and night, and they are always on time.

For many years the railroad runs smoothly. Then people stop using coal as fuel and the trains lose work … Finally, the train company runs out of money. The tunnels are closed up; most of the trains are taken away. The hidden world that lies under Chicago comes to an end.

The trains delivered their loads in two different ways. If a building had a deep basement, the train went straight into it. Otherwise, the freight cars were unhitched from the train and sent up to the building by elevator, one car at a time.

Ouch! She's stepping on my toe!

The railroad had its own police force. Policemen patrolled the tunnels and the areas where cars were loaded and unloaded.

The trains delivered coal, food, mail, and packages to stores, offices, and warehouses. They also hauled garbage away from these places. Sometimes the trains even carried visitors. Passengers rode in special cars fitted with benches.

23

An Underground Escape

It's a harsh winter night in Germany during World War II. The wind howls as it races through the prisoner-of-war camp. It hurls snow at the watchtowers manned by German guards, ready to shoot anyone they see trying to escape. Below the towers, prisoners wait in their huts, trying to stay warm and pretending that nothing

unusual is going to happen. They are about to escape through a secret tunnel they've been working on for many months.

It has been hard, dangerous work building a long tunnel under this prison camp, known as Stalag Luft III. The prisoners have only knives and small digging tools to carve an underground passage. They must

The entrance to Harry was hidden under a stove in a prisoners' hut. To get into Harry, prisoners moved the stove and climbed down a shaft they had dug.

Wood from the prisoners' beds propped up the soft, sandy walls.

Prisoners used stolen electrical wire to tap into the camp's power supply and light up the tunnel.

tunnel through sand that caves in and threatens to bury them alive.

But the prisoners are determined to dig their way out. Their tunnel, code-named "Harry," is almost as long as a football field. It runs from inside the camp to beyond the barbed-wire fence.

Tonight, seventy-six prisoners will crawl through Harry and walk away from the camp. Most of them will be captured again, but three will make it all the way back to their homes in Norway and England. With the help of Harry, these prisoners will finally be free.

Shhhh! The prisoners had to work quietly and dig deep underground, because the guards had buried microphones here to pick up any tunneling sounds.

The tunnel was narrow. There was just enough room for a large man to squeeze through Harry.

The prisoners made a tiny railway, complete with tracks. Little cars carried men and carted out sand. Workers, not an engine, pulled the little cars.

There wasn't enough air to breathe in the tunnel, so prisoners joined together empty milk cans to make a long tube (left) and pumped fresh air through it.

Amazing Mail Tunnels

The time is the present. A race is about to start outside the Main Post Office in the city of Prague. Three people, the contestants, wait impatiently. Each holds a small parcel that must be delivered to a castle nearby. They can use any means to get the packages there, and the one whose parcel reaches the castle first will be the winner. The signal to begin is given. The contestants leap into action.

One person jumps into a delivery van and roars off to the castle. But it's rush hour, and the van gets stuck in heavy traffic. It takes one hour for the driver to reach the castle and deliver the package.

Another contestant hops on a bicycle. He zips around the slow-moving cars, darts past the van, and arrives at the castle in 25 minutes.

The third contestant walks into the Main Post Office, where she works. She shuts her parcel inside a slim metal container, places it in a hatch, and presses a button. Whoosh! A powerful stream of air moves the container through tunnels that run under the city. Each tunnel is tiny, about the width of a small soup can.

Thwump! The container arrives at the castle. The entire trip has taken four minutes. Prague's mail tunnels may be more than a century old, but to this day they're still the fastest and most reliable way to send mail throughout the city.

I know the way to win. I'll just take this in . . .

During the tunnels' busiest time, about 30 years ago, one million items passed through them in a single year. These days the tunnels still handle more than 70,000 pieces of mail a year.

Money and important business papers also travel through the tunnels. Some people, it is said, have used the tunnels to send secret messages, love letters, and even food to other people.

26

More About Tunnels

One eastern mole is known to have dug a tunnel the length of seven cars in a single day!

There's no telling what some moles will do to get attention!

Dark, Cozy Mole Holes
(pages 6–7)

Eastern moles dig their tunnels in many parts of North America. In the United States, this mole's range extends east from Wyoming, South Dakota, and Texas, to Michigan, Massachusetts, Connecticut, and Rhode Island, and runs as far south as Florida. The northern boundary of its range is in southwestern Ontario; this is the only place in Canada where eastern moles live.

An Old Old Tunnel Tale
(pages 8–9)

Here is the route Theseus took to reach the Minotaur …

Make Way for the Water!
(pages 10–11)

The first aqueduct that carried water into Rome was built more than 2,000 years ago. Altogether, the ancient Romans built 11 main aqueducts to supply the city with the huge amounts of water it used each day.

Tunnels were an important feature of these aqueducts, and the ancient Romans preferred to use tunnels rather than bridges to carry water, wherever possible. One reason for this had to do with protecting the city of Rome from people who wanted to attack and invade it. One of the first things an enemy would do was try to find the city's water supply and cut it off – and without any water the people of Rome wouldn't be able to survive. The advantage of water tunnels was that they were hidden underground, so they were difficult to find and cut off. Compared with tunnels, bridges that carried water were easy for an enemy to spot – and easy to damage or destroy.

Find out more about ancient Rome at: www.pbs.org/wgbh/nova/lostempires/roman

Pyramid Secrets
(pages 12–13)

When the Caliph's men entered the Great Pyramid, they discovered that its tunnels were very small and cramped. The passageway that led down to the room at the bottom of the pyramid, for instance, was only about the height of a six-year-old kid – far too short for an adult to stand in. To get through this tunnel, al-Mamun's men had to crawl on their hands and knees.

However, there were some spacious areas inside the pyramid as well. The King's Chamber, the room where the Caliph's men found the king's empty stone coffin, was about six times the height of a man! Take a virtual tour at: www.pbs.org/wgbh/nova/pyramid/explore/khufustory.html

Attack the Castle!
(pages 14–15)

Sometimes the people who lived inside a castle were able to defend themselves from attackers by digging a tunnel. If the castle dwellers discovered the attackers' tunnel work early on, before it was completed, men from the castle would spring into action and quickly dig their own tunnel. This would run from the castle to the attackers' tunnel. The men from the castle would try to burrow their way directly into the enemy's tunnel, where they would surprise their attackers and defeat them during a very fierce and often deadly battle.

A World of Salt
(pages 16–17)

Just how big is the salt-filled world of Wieliczka? Its passageways and rooms run almost 200 miles (322 kilometers) through the earth, and stretch over nine different levels. The mine contains more than 2,000 chambers, many of them centuries old.

If you visit the mine today, you can take a tour and walk through some of the tunnels and rooms in the upper levels. But you'll be able to see only a very small section of the mine; most of Wieliczka is off-limits to visitors. Outsiders are not allowed in the lower levels, where miners still work, removing salt from deep in the ground.

Beneath Paris Streets ...
(pages 18–19)

The Paris Catacombs are a strange place, and you might expect it to have a strange-looking entrance too. However, there's nothing unusual about the way in to the catacombs. The entrance is an ordinary doorway, on an ordinary city street, right by a subway station. To reach the catacombs, you pass through the doorway, then walk down a long, winding stair-case with stone steps, all the way to the bottom. This takes you directly into the catacombs, beneath the streets of Paris.

A Shy Man Hides
(pages 20–21)

Were you able to find all the items that the Duke of Portland accidentally dropped in the tunnels? His umbrella, top hat, four handkerchiefs, and spare pair of socks are circled in the illustration on the right.

Tunnels for Tiny Trains
(pages 22–23)

Freight trains ran in the Chicago rail tunnels from 1906 until 1959, when the tunnels were finally closed up. During that time, hundreds of little trains used the tunnels each day. If you took all the trains that went through the tunnels in a single day and joined them together, you would have had a train that was more than 10 miles (16 kilometers) long!

Each tunnel was about the width of four kids standing side by side. A tall man standing on the ground could fit comfortably under the highest part of the tunnel's curved ceiling – but he would have had to hunch over while standing by the sides of the tunnel, to avoid bumping his head as the ceiling sloped down.

An Underground Escape
(pages 24–25)

The prisoners of Stalag Luft III began digging the "Harry" tunnel in 1943 and finally finished it in 1944. Tons of sand had to be taken out of the ground during tunnel building. The prisoners couldn't leave it above-ground, out in the open, because the Germans would have seen it; the sand was bright yellow and didn't blend in with anything on the ground's surface. And if the guards had spotted the sand, they would have known right away that the prisoners were trying to break free.

So the prisoners had to come up with places to hide the sand. One place was the gardens located on the grounds of the prison camp, which the Germans allowed the prisoners to take care of themselves. Prisoners who were nicknamed "penguins" carried the sand from the tunnels to the gardens in bags hidden under their clothing. Once the penguins were in the gardens, they slowly trickled the sand onto the ground while other prisoners who worked there used rakes to mix the sand into the soil so that it could not be seen.

Amazing Mail Tunnels
(pages 26–27)

Prague is not the only city with mail tunnels. Similar tunnels lie under the streets of Paris and Milan, among other places. New York City has mail tunnels too. They were built at the same time as the tunnels in Prague, during the late 1890s. Unlike Prague's tunnels, the ones in New York are no longer in use; the company that owned the tunnels stopped delivering mail through them in 1953. Other tunnels were built under Chicago and Philadelphia.

Index

Acknowledgments

I worked with a terrific team of people while making this book. Rick Wilks at Annick Press suggested the idea of a tunnels book, invited me to write it, and encouraged me to find my own way through the subject matter. I greatly appreciated his helpful feedback and enthusiastic support.

Sheryl Shapiro not only expertly designed this book, but coordinated the efforts of everyone involved, and ensured that we met our deadlines. I've worked with Sheryl before and, as in the past, I relied on her unflappable good spirits and her savvy trouble-shooting skills. She's a pleasure to work with and, without her, this book wouldn't have happened.

As well as digging up difficult-to-find visual references for the illustrator, Tina Forrester assisted me by tracking down elusive pieces of information. She also found experts on various tunnels and arranged for them to review the text and illustrations and verify that everything was correct. And Tina was the one who first came across the Prague mail tunnels and the Chicago train tunnels and proposed that they be included in this book. I thank her for all her important contributions.

My hat is off to illustrator Tina Holdcroft – she knew just the right way to condense everything I wanted to say about a particular tunnel and turn it into an informative and entertaining picture. Tina also contributed some wonderful captions – in all that she did, she made certain that the topic of tunnels was never musty or dull.

Many thanks, as well, to my husband, Michael, who is always supportive of my writing and who offered much encouragement when, periodically, I lost sight of the light at the end of the tunnel. And, finally, I must acknowledge my son, Benjamin. Benjamin plunged into the world of tunnels with great enthusiasm: he built tunnels out of his blocks, drew pictures of tunnels, and often sat with me, asking me many questions about tunnels, as I pored over books and websites about them. Benjamin never let me forget how interesting tunnels can be, and I hope I've made a book that he, and others, will enjoy.
—*Debora Pearson*

Many thanks to all the consultants and experts who contributed time, information, and reference photos. Special thanks to: Dr. Phil Myers, curator of the mammal section of the University of Michigan Zoology Museum in Ann Arbor, Michigan; Alison Easson, curator of the Greek and Roman collection at the Royal Ontario Museum in Toronto, Ontario; Paul Denis, a curator of Greek and Roman Byzantine art, also at the Royal Ontario Museum; the staff at the Wieliczka Salt Museum in Wieliczka, Poland; Dr. Nicholas Millett, senior curator of the Egyptian department at the Royal Ontario Museum; Phil O'Keefe from Chicago, Illinois, a mechanical engineer who specializes in railroad and industrial subjects, and a builder of detailed scale models for railroads, corporations, and museums; Stephen Shapiro from Toronto, Ontario, an aficionado of the Second World War; and Henry Hahn, philatelist from Fairfax, Virginia, with a special interest in the Prague pneumatic mail tunnels.
—*Tina Forrester*